ACKNOWLEDGEMENTS

Kathy McAteer (co-chair)
Joint Commissioning Manager
Sandwell Health Authority and Social Services Department

Gary McBrien (co-chair)
Planning Officer – Learning Disabilities
Birmingham Social Services Department

Carl Archer
Community Placement Officer
Birmingham Social Services Department

Miriam Darbyshire
Principal Assistant – Day Services
Staffordshire County Council

Paul Eggett
Sexuality Consultant
Freelance

Catherine Evers
Consultant Clinical Psychologist
Worcestershire Health Care NHS Trust

Mike Gunn
Head – Department of Academic Legal Studies
The Nottingham Trent University

Paul Jaunzems
General Manager
Langstone Society

Bridgit McClure
Community Nursing Manager – Learning Disabilities
Solihull Healthcare NHS Trust

Sue Marshall
Psychologist
Black Country Mental Health Trust

Mysie Raine
Team Manager
Herefordshire and Worcestershire County Social Services

Louise Rogers
Planning and Development Officer
Staffordshire County Council

Graham Tuckley
HIV Co-ordinator
Walsall Social Services Department

FOREWORD

The West Midlands Learning Disability Forum was established in 1985 to provide a regional focus for the development of new strategies and services for people with a learning disability. The Forum is supported by the West Midlands branch of the Association of Directors of Social Services and West Midlands Regional Health Authority.

The group meet regularly to share information, discuss and advise upon issues related to learning disabilities and to promote contact, discussion and communication with other disciplines.

Membership of the West Midlands Learning Disability Forum comprises representatives of the following services and organisations:

Barnardos

Birmingham Social Services

British Institute of Learning Disabilities

Central Council for Education & Training in Social Work

Coventry Social Services

Dudley Social Services

Hereford Social Services

Mencap

National Autistic Society

North Staffordshire Health Authority

Sandwell Social Services

Shropshire Social Services

Social Services Inspectorate

Solihull Social Services

South Warwickshire Health Authority

Staffordshire Social Services

Walsall Social Services

Warwickshire Social Services

West Midlands Association of the Directors of Social Services

West Midlands Regional Health Authority

Wolverhampton Social Services

Worcester Social Services

INTRODUCTION

In 1992 the West Midlands Learning Disability Forum (WMLDF) published a policy statement and guidelines for staff working with adults with learning disabilities regarding social and personal relationships. This was adopted and used by the majority of social service departments and organisations within the West Midlands providing services to people with learning disabilities.

As a consequence of the changes in legislation and the developments in services for adults with learning disabilities the WMLDF decided in 1997 to revise the original policy statement and guidelines. A multi-agency group was established and agreed to produce a Policy Statement and Good Practice Guidelines, which aim to:

Section 1
Provide a policy framework which outlines the rights and responsibilities of staff, carers, relatives and adults with learning disabilities.

Section 2
Provide guidance on how the policy can be used by staff in various settings, in supporting adults with learning disabilities in their social and personal relationships.

SECTION 1

Policy Statement

SECTION 1 – POLICY STATEMENT

It is recommended that Authorities and other care providers should have in place a policy for staff working with adults with learning disabilities regarding personal and social relationships. This policy framework is intended to assist Authorities who may either wish to adopt the policy and guidance or use it as a basis for developing their own.

Why do we need a policy?

The need for a policy about our own social and personal relationships would be totally unacceptable to all of us. These relationships are a very important and private part of our lives. However, we all have rights and responsibilities in terms of how we conduct our social and personal relationships and we all act within some constraints including being subject to current legislation.

Adults with learning disabilities have the same rights and responsibilities as everyone else. They may however also need support with various parts of their lives including developing social and personal relationships and in understanding their rights and responsibilities.

Staff and carers, in supporting adults with learning disabilities in developing social and personal relationships, will often feel they are intruding into private and sensitive areas of their lives. They will often be working with other staff, carers and adults with learning disabilities who hold a range of views on social and personal relationships.

Staff and carers may find themselves supporting adults with learning disabilities with sensitive issues and dilemmas regarding their relationships where there are no easy answers.

Staff and carers will equally be concerned with balancing the rights of adults with learning disabilities to develop social and personal relationships and protecting individuals who might be at risk of abuse and exploitation.

This policy is written to support staff in working with adults with learning disabilities in developing their social and personal relationships. It endeavours to describe the rights, responsibilities and risks in relation to social and personal relationships for an adult with learning disabilities, their carers/relatives, staff and organisations. It is not designed to deal with situations where staff, carers or adults with learning disabilities feel a person with learning disabilities is at risk of being abused or exploited. In those circumstances adult protection policies/procedures should be used. It is intended that this policy will benefit staff, adults with learning disabilities and their carers by meeting their mutual interests.

Social and Personal Relationships

We all have a need for social and personal relationships; the strength of that need and the way in which it is expressed will be different for each person.

Whilst someone with a learning disability may have frequent contact with people such as family members, they may not be able to develop other relationships. This might be due to them having restricted choices or opportunities, parental attitudes, lack of privacy and high support needs.

As with other people it is important for adults with learning disabilities to be able to develop a range and variety of relationships. These relationships may therefore include social relationships with acquaintances and more permanent friendships. They may include a range of sexual relationships including same sex relationships. They may include marriage or living with a partner. There will also be issues for people with learning disabilities who are over 16 years of age but are not yet legally adults over the age of 18.

Rights and Responsibilities

Adults with learning disabilities have the same rights to freedom and choice in what they do within the bounds of their society and its laws as everyone else. As a first principle, adults with learning disabilities should be treated as having equal rights. Issues of consent, mental incapacity and the Mental Health Act 1983 can be applied to all citizens.

Implict in this statement is that everyone has a responsibility to respect the rights of others to freedom and choice. Staff must respect these rights whilst ensuring that a person with learning disabilities is not open to abuse or exploitation.

The following is a set of guiding principles, which have already been tested and used within Personal Relationships Advisory Groups, to help solve difficult problems that have come up for staff, service providers and adults with learning disabilities.

Adults with learning disabilities have the following rights:
- Access to guidance which will assist them in their social, personal and sexual development

- Access to support and advice from people who are competent to provide it

- The right to be assisted in pursuing the type of social and personal relationships they want

- The opportunity to develop close, intimate and loving relationships and the privacy which this demands

- To have appropriate support and protection from exploitation, abuse and degrading treatment

- To have information about himself/herself kept confidential

- To have accessible information/explanation in order to make an informed choice

- To have an advocate, someone to speak on his/her behalf if wanted

- To be treated with respect, consideration and sensitivity

- To be given support and assistance to make a complaint if they feel their rights have not been upheld.

Adults with learning disabilities have the following responsibilities:
- To receive advice and information appropriate to their needs

- To stay within the law as any other citizen

- To respect the rights of others

- To treat others with respect, consideration and sensitivity

Carers/Relatives have the following rights: *(This does not include a paid member of staff)*
Though carers and relatives do not have any legal rights over the affairs of an adult with learning disabilities, their influence will often be a crucial factor and needs to be acknowledged. Carers and relatives do however have some rights and expectations of their own which need to be taken into account:

- To be clear about their role and the support available to them

- To be informed and consulted if the adult with learning disabilities has clearly expressed this as their wish

- To make representation on behalf of the adult with learning disabilities and themselves

- To be treated with respect, consideration and sensitivity

- To advice and support from relevant agencies

- Not to be held responsible for the action of the adult with learning disabilities

- To be given support and assistance to make a complaint if their rights/ expectations or the rights of the adult with learning disabilities have not been upheld

Carers/Relatives have the following responsibilities:

- To work constructively with others involved in supporting the adult with learning disabilities as agreed in the care plan or any other agreement

- To treat their relative/adult with learning disabilities with respect and consideration

- To make a distinction between what is in the best interest of their relative/ person with a learning disability and what is in their own best interest

- To offer a safe and supportive environment which provides appropriate opportunities for risk taking

- To keep the services supporting them informed where appropriate

- To support the adult with learning disabilities in seeking information and advice where appropriate

Staff and managers have the following rights:

- To be given relevant information, advice, support, supervision, and training from someone who is appropriately skilled and conversant with policy on personal and social relationships

- To be treated with respect, consideration and sensitivity

- To be protected from unfair allegations and adverse publicity and supported when allegations are made by means of policies and procedures

Staff and managers have the following responsibilities:

- To work constructively with others within policies and procedures to support adults with learning disabilities in pursuing personal and social relationships

- To report any incidents of abuse, neglect or poor practice in line with their employers' adult protection procedures

- To make appropriate use of supervision and information given

- To seek information and advice

- To support the adult with learning disabilities, and provide them with relevant and appropriate information

- To ensure that the adult with learning disabilities is kept informed and treated with respect and dignity in a non-abusive environment

- To ensure that the law is adhered to and any necessary clarification sought

- To make decisions appropriate to their status in the organisation

- To actively promote best practice according to the value base, policy and guidelines of the service

- To participate in on-going training to help achieve these responsibilities and aims.

SECTION 2

Good Practice Guidelines

Section 2

Practice Guidelines

Contents

I. THE LAW

Introduction

All care staff are rightly concerned about the legal implications of supporting people with a disability in matters of personal and legal relationships. In a field as yet virtually untried in case law, each employing authority is entitled to its own view, which means that any case brought to law is likely to be tried on its own merits. (Craft 1982).

In fact, prosecutions under the following Acts have been rare and commonly failed.

The law acts as a safeguard protecting the 'vulnerable' from the 'unscrupulous', but where it can be shown that the service provided is, in professional judgement, a positive aid to the person, it would be expected to protect those providing such services.

Terminology

The term 'mental handicap' is often used in legal terms, to mean people with a learning disability.

It should be noted that the term 'severe mental handicap' is used in some legislation whereas other legislation uses 'defective'. The term 'defective' is defined as a person suffering from a state of arrested or incomplete development of mind which includes severe impairment of intelligence and social functioning. For the purposes of working with adults with learning disabilities these mean the same thing. The term 'learning disability' has no legal meaning.

The Relevant Acts

1. The Sexual Offences Act 1956, Section 7, makes it an offence subject to certain exceptions for a man to have unlawful sexual intercourse with a woman who is 'a defective'. A man charged may, in his defence, claim he did not know or had no reason to suspect her to be 'a defective'. The term 'defective' is defined as a person suffering from a state of arrested or incomplete development of mind which includes severe impairment of intelligence and social functioning.

2. Section 128 of the Mental Health Act 1959 makes it an offence for a man to have unlawful sexual intercourse with a woman suffering from any form of mental disorder, if the man is a manager of, or on the staff of a hospital or

residential nursing home at which the woman is an inpatient or to have such intercourse on the premises of any part of that hospital or home with a woman who is for the time being receiving such treatment there as an out-patient. This applies to **any** mental disorder.

Section 128 of the Mental Health Act 1959 also makes it an offence for a man to have unlawful sexual intercourse with a woman who is a mentally disordered patient and who is subject to his guardianship under the Mental Health Act 1983, or is otherwise in his custody and care under the Mental Health Act 1983, or in pursuance of arrangements under Part 3 of the National Assistance Act 1948 or the National Health Service Act 1977, or is a resident in a residential care home within the meaning of Part 1 of the Registered Homes Act 1984.

3. Section 1(3) of the Sexual Offences Act 1967 states that a man suffering from 'severe mental handicap', within the meaning of the Act, cannot in law give 'consent' to homosexual acts.

   Section 1(2) tells us that sexual behaviour between more than two men would be deemed illegal.

4. The Sexual Offences Act 1956, Section 14, makes reference to a woman who is a defective being unable to consent to an indecent assault. The term 'defective' is given exactly the same meaning as quoted above. Section 15(3) of the Sexual Offences Act 1956 refers to a defective man being unable to consent to an indecent assault and again 'defective' is given the same meaning as quoted above.

5. It is prohibited for a person to procure a 'severely mentally handicapped' woman for the purposes of unlawful intercourse (Section 9, Sexual Offences Act 1956).

6. All people are entitled to marry and their marriage will be regarded as valid as long as it can be shown that they understood the nature and responsibilities of the 'contract' into which they were entering. If either party did not give valid consent, the marriage is voidable, meaning it may be ended at the wish of either party. Under Section 12(d) of the Matrimonial Causes Act 1973, a marriage is voidable if '*at the time of the marriage either party, though capable of giving valid consent, was suffering (whether continuously or intermittently) from mental disorder within the meaning of the Mental Health Act 1959, of such a kind or to such an extent as to be unfitted for marriage*'.

   This is rarely used as a ground for annulment.

7.   Section 27 of the Sexual Offences Act 1956 makes it an offence for the owner or manager of any premises to induce or allow a 'severely mentally handicapped' woman to be on the premises for the purpose of having unlawful sexual intercourse with a man.

8.   Staff should keep in mind that it is an offence to assist the commission of a crime which may arise even if a member of staff does not himself/herself commit one of the crimes referred to above.

Section 28

This is Section 28 of the Local Government Act 1988 which came into force in May 1988. The section prohibits elected members of a local authority from intentionally promoting homosexuality or from publishing material with the intention of promoting homosexuality, or promoting the teaching in any maintained school of the acceptability of homosexuality as a 'pretended family relationship'. Material relating to homosexuality within the context of a sex education programme will not be seen as a breach of the Act or in any way promoting homosexuality.

Reading

Gunn, M J; (1996); **Sex and the Law**; (4th Edition); Family Planning Association, London.

The British Medical Association and the Law Society; (BMA/LSD 1995); **Assessment of Mental Capacity: Guidance for Doctors and Lawyers**; BMA, London.

The Mental Health Acts 1959 and 1983.

If concerns remain
Seek legal advice from your agency's legal section.

2. CONSENT

Underpinning knowledge

In relation to adults over the age of 18 (16 for medical treatment) the law assumes that adults have the mental capacity to make their own decisions and have the capacity to consent. The Law Commission has stated that people should be enabled and encouraged to take for themselves those decisions which they are able to take. There are certain circumstances when the right of an adult to make his/her own decision is taken away. This is when the adult is considered not to have sufficient understanding to make the decision and is regarded as lacking legal capacity. Under the Sexual Offences legislation there is no interest in an individual's capacity if s/he is 'a defective' or has a 'severe mental handicap', because, if that condition exists, his/her consent is legally invalid. For other people with a learning disability, the general restrictions on sexual activity in relation to age and consent apply as they do to all other people.

An adult cannot be deemed incompetent to make a decision about one part of their life, simply because they have been incompetent in other areas. Each decision regarding capacity can only relate to that particular decision-making area. Many people with learning disabilities have never experienced full choice and control over their lives. The law, the practice of service organisations, and public opinion have in the past sometimes endorsed the idea that people with learning disabilities are not able to make decisions for themselves and need protecting for their own good. This is no longer considered appropriate.

There is further information on the law as it affects people with learning disabilities and those labelled as being 'defective' or 'severely mentally handicapped' as defined in the Sexual Offences Act 1956 and 1967 regarding their sexual and personal relationships in Section 1 of the guidance.

Key Principles

Where two people with learning disabilities develop a sexual relationship and appear to be happy with it and there is no evidence of exploitation, many professionals would consider that it would not be reasonable to interrupt the relationship, despite the fact that it may be difficult to establish the capacity to consent. Nevertheless this is a difficult decision in which those involved with the couple need to consider the risks to the individuals as well as their rights. Remember that there are only special legal rules in relation to sexual relationships/activity where the person in question is a 'defective' or has a 'severe mental handicap' under the 1956 and 1967 Sexual Offences Act.

Those involved with the people should:

- document their decisions carefully;

- include those closest to the individual, who are familiar with the individual's usual pattern of communication (not just a medical practitioner), including an independent advocate;

- allow sufficient time, in an appropriate location for an assessment to take place (one assessment meeting may well not be enough);

- include all available and relevant information;

The decisions should:

- be justifiable by those who make the assessment;

- be open to a simple system of challenge.

The person's potential to make a decision for themselves should be maximised and this includes effective language and communication skills by those trying to ascertain whether the individual can make the decision. This is a crucial point for people with learning disabilities, some of whom do not use speech and many of whom are easily excluded from decision-making by complicated language and concepts.

All practical steps to communicate with, and involve, people must be used and include:

- the use of appropriate words, pictures and symbols;

- involving people skilled in using these techniques;

- involving people close to the individual and familiar with their ways of communicating;

- a suitable environment and enough time for the communication to take place.

Where there are concerns about adults with learning disabilities who may be engaged in abusive relationships, there are a number of issues which should be considered.

These include for example:

- whether there is a power imbalance between the two people;

- whether tangible inducements have been used by one person;

- whether, in the case of heterosexual relationships, the people involved know about the risk of pregnancy;

- whether both partners know about safer sex and are able to use this knowledge.

The greatest possible care must be given to establishing (full) consent to a sexual relationship for a person with learning disabilities, not only because that reflects what is in their best interest, but also because it minimises any likely legal intervention. However, staff should be cautious of using the duty of care (see Section 1) to deny people choice.

Training

An understanding about consent issues should be included in the general training provided for staff, especially in the induction pack.

Reading

Gunn, M J; (1996); **Sex and the Law**; (4th Edition); Family Planning Association, London. This book provides a comprehensive guide to the law relating to sex and people with learning disabilities.

The British Medical Association and The Law Society; (BMA/AL 1995) **Assessment of Mental Capacity: Guidance for Doctors and Lawyers**. BMA, London.

Law Commission; (1995); **Mental Incapacity (Report no. 231)**; HMSO, London

Murphy, G; Clare, I C H; (1997); **Consent Issues in Adults with Learning Disabilities**; J O' Hara and A Sperlinger (Eds); John Wiley and Son Ltd.

Murphy, G; Clare, I C H; (1995); **Adults' capacity to make decisions affecting the person**; Psychologists contribution in R Bull and D Carson) (Eds) Handbook of Psychology in legal context. Chichester. John Wiley and Son; pages 97 – 128

Murphy, G; (1997); **Defining sexual abuse, consent and duty to report in There are no easy answers**; Churchill J; Brown H; Craft A; Horrocks C; (Eds); Pages 30-33.

My Choice, My Own Choice (Video);

It's only natural (Video);

Handbook of Psychology in Legal Contexts; (1998); Bull, R, Carson, D; (Eds.).

If concerns remain

If concerns regarding the issue of consent to sexual relationships remain, you may wish to consider the following:

- a risk assessment;

- a multidisciplinary discussion concerning the issue, and/or

- referral to an advisory group within the agency;

- referral to an expert outside the agency.

3. RISK

Underpinning knowledge

Freedom of choice means freedom within reason to take risks. Responsible risk-taking must be accepted as a normal part of daily living and this includes matters of personal choice. Freedom of choice means we all take risks on the basis of informed choice and make personal decisions about what we deem to be an acceptable risk.

Key Principles

- All actions of staff must encourage the exercise of choice as a feature of normal life and as a means of expressing individuality, self-respect and mutual support.

- When a comprehensive assessment has been carried out, elements involving risk-taking will have been explored, discussed and incorporated in the Individual Programme Plan or Care Plan.

- It is, however, acknowledged that in some circumstances there may be conflict between the individual and their carer regarding their understanding of the degree of risk involved in certain activities. In these situations a formal case review should take place with all appropriate people involved to achieve overall agreement. If persistent conflict continues, it may be advisable to involve an independent advocate.

- People should not be discouraged from undertaking certain activities solely on the grounds that there may be an element of risk. Watchfulness and preparation are better than over-protectiveness. Staff should work towards consensus with individuals and their carers in assessing competence to judge risks.

- Comprehensive recording must be made regarding any discussions and decisions and included in the individual's Care Plan. However, it is the individual's wishes which should be paramount.

- The encouragement of choice should never mean an abdication of responsibility on behalf of the staff. *We should always remember we have a duty of care.*

Training

Risk assessments in line with employer's procedures. Induction training should address issues relating to decision making and consent.

Reading

Morgan, S; **Assessing and Managing Risk**; A training pack for practitioners and managers of Comprehensive Mental Health Services. Pavillion 1998. The Sainsbury Centre for Mental Health.

Moore, B; (1996); **Risk Assessment: A Practitioner's Guide to Predicting Harmful Behaviour**; Whiting and Birch Ltd.

If concerns remain

Where staff have concerns about the support they receive, they should contact their line manger or other appropriate person (someone you feel comfortable with – this may be another manager within the department, staff counsellor, trade union representative or your professional body).

4. ADVOCACY

Underpinning knowledge

Advocacy – Working Definition:
The representation and pursuit of the rights of another as if they were your own

Advocacy refers to the process of pleading the cause and/or acting on behalf of another person (or persons) to secure the services they require and/or rights to which they are entitled. This includes the right to ask, question, be heard and receive answers even if an outcome remains unaltered. Advocates owe those they represent a duty of loyalty, confidentiality and a commitment to be zealous in the promotion of their cause.

There are different types of advocacy. Most advocacy schemes consist of trained, selected volunteers and co-ordinating staff who work on behalf of those who have a disability/are disadvantaged and not in a good position to exercise or defend their rights as citizens. Advocates are independent of those providing services.

Key Principles

All service users should be offered advocacy from someone who is separate from the provider of the service. This should incorporate the following key principles.

Unpaid
Advocates are normally unpaid and choose to spend time with their partner. This is a very strong part of the partnership and means that time spent together is not restricted but negotiated between the advocate and partner they choose.

No Conflict of Interest
By offering independent support from outside the normal framework of services, advocates are able to pursue an issue further than a paid worker could. The person requiring support, the 'partner', may also feel more comfortable discussing some concerns with an independent person.

Confidential
Advocates are not as restricted as staff in making promises of confidentiality to an individual and will not share information unless their partner has expressly requested them to do so. However, advocates should work to guidelines regarding harmful or illegal behaviour or disclosures of abuse etc.

One to One
Most advocacy partnerships will be between two individuals; the 'advocate', normally a volunteer, and the 'partner', the person requiring support. The

advocate is able to give all their energy and commitment to one person in a way that staff from other agencies often cannot.

Partner-led

Advocates accept that it is their partner who chooses what they wish to do and that they are the experts in their own situation. An advocate is non-directive in their approach but will discuss options, possible consequences and risks. The partner retains maximum control and an advocate takes no action without the express permission of the partner. An advocate has no particular rights or authority to personal or confidential information unless with their partner's permission.

Partner Loyalty

Whereas workers may need to be 'loyal' to 'the total' of their clients, an advocate is able to set their partner before any other individual or agency.

Open-ended

Advocacy partnerships last as long as both parties wish. This can be until a particular issue is resolved or even a lifetime depending on the individuals concerned.

Training

As they are independent organisations, advocacy schemes vary in the ways in which they operate. Most schemes are very welcoming of enquiries about their work and will supply leaflets and information on request.

Many organisations will be happy to given presentations and meet with staff to explain their work.

Although there is no national body for advocacy schemes, a national list of schemes is available from:

Citizen Advocacy & Training (CAT)
Unit 164
Lee Valley Technopark
Ashley Road
Tottenham
London
N17 9LN

Tel: 020 8880 4545/4546
Fax: 020 8880 4113
E-mail: cait@leevalley.co.uk
Website: www.leevalley.co.uk/cait

Reading

Beresford, P; Croft, S; (1993) **Citizen Involvement: A Practical Guide for Change**; Macmillan.

Brandon, D; (1995) **Advocacy: More Power to Disabled People**; Venture Press, Birmingham.

UK Advocacy Network; (1994); **Advocacy: A Code of Practice**; UKAN

Williams, P; (1998); **Standing by Me**; CAIT, London.

Winn, L; (Ed) (1993); **Power to the People**; King's Fund.

If concerns remain

The vast majority of schemes will have a paid manager or co-ordinator who would want to hear of any concerns regarding advocates supported by their scheme. The scheme should also have a formal complaints procedure which you may request if appropriate.

5. STAFF SUPPORT

Underpinning knowledge

It is of paramount importance that any agency has a framework in place for providing advice and support to staff at all levels (including managers) who deal with difficult and sensitive situations.

This is particularly important given the vulnerability of staff in relation to supporting and advising people in matters of sexuality.

Key Principles

- For agencies to consider setting up an Advisory Group to work across agencies with external input from an independent person. In the absence of an Advisory Group, agencies should ensure that staff can receive support from someone external to the agency.

- Agencies should put in place a formal process to involve staff in agreeing 'house rules' or 'service rules' within the setting in which they work, regarding sexual or intimate behaviour. This may include, for example, issues regarding toilets as public places within day centres, or behaviour which others may find offensive in a public place.

Training

- To provide basic personal relationship/sexuality training to all staff working with people with learning disabilities

- To provide specialist in-depth training for those who provide support and advice to colleagues

Reading/Resources

Further information can be obtained from 'Personal Relationships Advisory Groups' Brighton and Sandwell Social Services Departments.

If concerns remain

Where staff have concerns about the support they receive, they should contact their line manger or other appropriate person (someone you feel comfortable with – this may be another manager within the department, staff counsellor, trade union representative or your professional body).

6. TRAINING

Underpinning knowledge

Training is seen as an essential pre-requisite to any work undertaken with people with a learning disability. All staff are expected to have a basic understanding of the issues around personal relationships for this client group and training is seen as vitally important in facilitating this.

Key Principles

- All newly appointed staff as part of their induction need to have an awareness of the guidelines produced by the employer and at an individual establishment or service level.

  These include:

  - Confidentiality

  - Equal opportunities

  - Rights of individuals

  - Physical contact/practical aspects of day to day care

  - Department guidelines in relation to Vulnerable Adults Policy including local implementation

  - Resource available to assist and support individuals

- Individual training needs should be an integral part of ongoing staff supervision.

- All staff to have opportunities made available to access further in-depth training in all aspects of Personal and Social Relationships, as reflected in NVQ training.

Reading

McCarthy, M; Thompson, D; **Sexuality, Sexual Abuse and Safer Sex: Training Manual for staff working with People with Learning Difficulties.**

Craft, A; **Sexuality and Learning Disabilities.**

Gunn, M J; (1996); **Sex and the Law**; (4th Edition); Family Planning Association, London.

Life Skills Training Manual Set (Set 2, Personal Safety and Personal Care); Winslow Press.

Craft, A; **Sexual Counselling for Mentally Handicapped People, their Parents and Care Staff.**

If concerns remain

Where staff have concerns about the support they receive, they should contact their line manger or other appropriate person (someone you feel comfortable with – this may be another manager within the department, staff counsellor, trade union representative or your professional body).

7. EQUAL OPPORTUNITIES

Underpinning knowledge

It is commonly recognised that there are groups of people in our society that are socially excluded groups. These groups of people may be denied access to facilities, services and employment opportunities. Members from socially excluded groups may have very individual needs in the area of personal and social relationships and care must be taken to ensure equity of service provision in addressing the individual's need.

Key Principles

- Common prejudice and discrimination have been identified in the following areas:

  - Race/ethnic origin

  - Creed

  - Age

  - Gender

  - Marital status

  - Class

  - Sexual orientation

  - Health

  - Disability

- Before undertaking work with any individual, staff should familiarise themselves with issues around discrimination and individual needs of the person.

Training

- All agencies should have in place policies regarding the following:

  - Anti oppressive practice

- Anti discrimination issues

- Equal opportunities

● All staff should be provided with training in respect of the above.

Reading

Employer's Policy and Procedures Manual

If concerns remain

Where staff feel that equal opportunities are not an integral part of service delivery they should discuss these concerns with their line manager or another appropriate person (someone you feel comfortable with – this may be another manager within the department, or your professional body).

8. CONFIDENTIALITY

Underpinning knowledge

Issues around a person's personal and sexual relationships are a confidential matter requiring sensitivity and respect. The way in which staff manage personal information should reflect this. However, staff should never offer total confidentiality to anyone as personal information may have to be passed to a third party e.g. where an allegation of abuse is made.

Key Principles

- If personal information is to be passed on, good practice normally requires that the consent of the person providing the information is sought. There are circumstances where information can be passed without the person's consent e.g. investigation of serious crimes.

- Irrespective of whether consent is given or not it is important that the person has clear understanding of why the information is being passed on and to whom. It may be necessary to employ an advocate for this purpose.

- Staff should refer to any professional codes of practice and policies laid down by their employer in respect of access to information and recording procedures.

Training

- An understanding about issues of confidentiality should be included in general staff training specifically in the induction pack/training.

Reading

Employer's Policy and Procedures Manual

If concerns remain
If concerns remain regarding confidentiality, staff should discuss and seek advice from their line manager or supervisor.

9. WHISTLE BLOWING

Underpinning knowledge

It is recommended that employers establish a system whereby people can express concerns about a colleague's professionalism as part of improving quality standards. (This will include physical, financial, sexual and emotional abuse as well as neglect.)

Key Principles

- Any systems would need to consider inclusion of the following:

    - Confidentiality

    - Neutrality

    - Respect and support for the person reporting the allegation and for them to be informed about the outcome of the investigation

    - Introduction of procedures to support the victim during and after the investigation

    - Systems if allegations prove false or mischievous

    - Systems for monitoring – recognition of signs of abuse.

Training

- An understanding of whistle-blowing and procedures to be followed should be included in induction pack and training.

Reading

Employer's Policy and Procedure Manual

Employer's Adult Abuse Procedures on Vulnerable Adults Policy

Public Interest Disclosure Act 1998

Guidance for SSDs on the Abuse of People with Learning Disabilities in Independent Care ADSS/NAPSAC

If concerns remain

Where staff have concerns about the support they receive, they should contact their line manger or other appropriate person (someone you feel comfortable with – this may be another manager within the department, staff counsellor, trade union representative or your professional body).

10. PARENTAL/CARER INVOLVEMENT

Underpinning knowledge

The majority of people with learning disabilities continue to live with parents or other close family carers and the influence and importance of those relationships cannot be underestimated. It is also important to recognise the cultural diversity of individuals and their families which may influence decision-making and values and attitudes.

Key Principles

It is important to recognise that parents and carers of people with learning disabilities have no legal say in what their adult relative does. The law does not recognise the ability of anyone to give consent on behalf of another person. However, it must be recognised that parents and carers often have an influence, a sense of responsibility, and may have extreme difficulty coming to terms with their relative's approach to their personal relationships and their sexuality. It would be important to ensure that they are part of a process to decide the capacity to consent, if in question, of their relative.

People involved with people with learning disabilities need to be realistic and accept that family relationships are unique in every situation. It is preferable to initiate contact with carers rather than respond to anxieties on a crisis basis. Parents/carers should only participate in discussion about personal and sexual relationships where the individual concerned has given permission to do so. This should only be undertaken in private with the individual's confidante, key worker or advocate. There may be times when the person cannot give informed permission or agreement (see Part 2 Consent and Part 3 Risk).

It is suggested that when service users join any service (day centres, residential accommodation, etc) a leaflet should be given to them and parents/carers. This would clearly set out the service's position and policies on a range of issues which, of course, would include the development of social and personal relationships. This should include an explanation of the rights of the individuals and a philosophy statement from the service.

Parents/carers should be offered opportunities to comment and be involved in the development of education/ information about personal and social relationships for people with learning disabilities. Information about such areas should be available to parents/carers before their relative starts to receive a service.

Training

All staff need to be aware of the potential tension between the various people involved in the care of a person with learning disabilities. This awareness should be included in an induction pack and training should be on-going.

If concerns remain

A service may wish to develop an explicit framework which sets out clearly what the different relationships are between the service and the parents/carers and the service and the service user. It is important to achieve a balance between parental/carer involvement whilst ensuring the needs of the person with learning disabilities are also met. For example, your service may decide that parents have the right to information but service users have the rights to confidentiality. This may need to be clearly stated in service information.

11. PERSONAL & SEXUAL RELATIONSHIPS

Underpinning knowledge

Staff need to be aware of the law, policy and good practice that governs their work. They need to know why relationships are important to people as well as the reasons for encouraging and developing these. Whilst some individuals will need support in developing and maintaining relationships, others will not. It is the individual's perception of their sexuality which is important and the manner in which they express this within a social situation. This expression can vary and change according to relationships and contexts.

Staff should be aware of the concept of self-image and identity. Staff should actively encourage people to take an interest in, and express feelings about, themselves.

Key Principles

- Work with people regarding their personal and sexual relationships must be within the boundaries of confidentiality and privacy.

- Workers' behaviour should be consistent and non-exploitative.

- Workers will need to be aware of their own beliefs and values and how these may impact on their own behaviour.

- It is important to be aware of the assumptions which surround sex and sexuality and for staff to understand the reasons why it is important not to make assumptions about individuals.

- Individuals should be encouraged to recognise their own rights and responsibilities.

- Staff should be aware of the sources of support and guidance in relation to working with people in respect of their personal and sexual relationships. Staff should be made aware of the action to take should they encounter situations in which they feel unable to cope.

Training

National/Scottish Vocational Qualification Frameworks include specific elements of competence in relation to personal and sexual relationships.

Training based on Normalisation or Social Role Valorisation usually includes consideration of an individual's self-image and identity. Although issues of sexuality may not be explicitly addressed, such issues have relevant connections.

If concerns remain

Where staff have concerns about the support they receive, they should contact their line manager or other appropriate person (someone you feel comfortable with – this may be another manager within the department, staff counsellor, trade union representative or your professional body).

12. SEX EDUCATION

Underpinning knowledge

People should have full rights and responsibilities as regards their personal relationship and sexuality including the right to:

- Receive structured education about human development including sexuality and to be helped to develop a positive self-image of themselves.

- Learn to communicate about sexuality and to develop the appropriate language (including non-verbal) and the vocabulary to do so.

- The right to be given information, advice and guidelines on inappropriate sexual behaviour that might be socially, culturally or legally unacceptable;

- To be taught about sexual exploitation, i.e. to be aware of situations when they are at risk of exploitation or of exploiting others. Such teaching or training should include both information and skill development.

- The right to information about help with contraception and safer sex. This should be done in such a way as not to impose over-protective attitudes.

Key Principles

- It is important that care workers are aware of the law which particularly affects service users with learning disabilities. (See Part 1).

- It should be recognised that this is a sensitive area for all and that we have to avoid our personal, cultural, ethical, moral and/or religious views conflicting with the interests of others. It is impossible to be entirely neutral when discussing or teaching value-laden topics, but good practice dictates that every effort should be made to minimise the effects of personal attitudes. There should be no expectation that a staff member shall be required to change their own cultural, ethical, moral and/or religious codes. However, where these prevent a staff member from being directly involved in aspects of the agreed programme, they would still be expected to offer their support to other staff dealing with these issues.

- Staff need to be aware that some people may find sex education material sexually stimulating (see Part 24).

Training

- Staff should receive training around sexuality issues.

- Staff who have a role in delivering sex education should receive additional specific training.

Reading

Craft, A; (1994); **Living your Life**. A sex education and personal development programme for students with severe learning difficulties. (Handbook for teachers and tutors), Learning Development Aids, Wisbech.

Craft, A: Downs, C; (1997); **Sex in Context, parts 1 and 2**; Pavilion Publishing/Joseph Rowntree Foundation.

My Choice: My Own Choice; (1996); (Video) A resource which looks at issues of Sexuality and Sexual Health; Sexual Health team, Barnardos, Queens Road, Bradford.

It's Only Natural; (Video) For parents and Carers and Others involved in the lives of Young People with Learning Disabilities.

Hazelhurst, M; (1993); **Breaking in . . . breaking out. Social and sex education for men with learning disabilities**; Working with Men and the B Team; London.

Hollins, S; (1994); **Hug Me – Touch me**; The Sovereign Series, London.

Landman, R; (1994); **Let's talk about sex?** Health Promotion Service, Birmingham.

McCarthy, M; Thompson, D; (Revised 1998); **Sex and the three Rs. Rights, responsibilities and risks: A sex education package for working with people with learning difficulties**. Pavilion Publishing, Hove.

Atkinson, D; Gingell, A; Martin, J; (1996); **I have the right to know**; British Institute of Learning Disabilities, Kidderminster.

Contacts

Brook Advisory Centre, 9 York Road, Edgbaston, Birmingham B69 9HX
Tel: 0121 455 0491

SPOD, 286 Camden Road, London, N7 0BJ. Tel: 020 7607 8851/2

Family Planning Association, 27–35 Mortimer Street, London, W1N 7RJ

13. PERSONAL AND SEXUAL RELATIONSHIPS BETWEEN STAFF AND SERVICE USERS

Underpinning knowledge

It is an offence for male staff to have sexual intercourse with a woman in his care (please see Part 1 'The Law' for more details). Furthermore, it is always a disciplinary offence for a member of staff to seek or engage in intimate or sexual relationships with service users.

Key Principles

1. Relationships that are thought to be at risk of or have already extended beyond what may be considered to be professional are not acceptable. The Care Plan should inform the relationship between the members of staff and the service user.

2. Intimate or sexual relationships between staff and service users are **NOT** permissible. Staff are employed to provide professional support to users and intimate or sexual relationships are unequal and highly damaging.

3. All staff should be informed of the seriousness of breaching codes of conduct at the start of their employment, including being made aware of the organisation's disciplinary proceedings.

4. Managers have a responsibility to ensure that staff are not put in a position whereby they are isolated or vulnerable to their behaviour being misinterpreted by a service user or others.

5. Staff have a responsibility not to put themselves in a position of vulnerability and to be aware of how their behaviour may be interpreted.

Training

- staff education programme

- information provided as part of induction pack

Further Reading

It's only natural; (Video) For Parents, Carers and Others involved in the lives of Young People with Learning Disabilities.

My Choice: My Own Choice; (1996); (Video) A resource which looks at issues of Sexuality and Sexual Health; Sexual Health Team, Barnardos, Queens Road, Bradford.

Gunn, M J; (1996); **Sex and the Law**; (4th Edition); Family Planning Association, London.

If concerns remain
A risk assessment should be undertaken immediately.

14. SENSUALITY

Underpinning knowledge

Sensuality can be defined as gratification of the senses. It is an important part of quality of life for people with learning disabilities. People working with people with learning disabilities might fall in to the trap of stripping out aspects of sensuality from the experience of people with learning disabilities in the name of protection. It is important to examine our own understanding of sensuality and safe working practices and then develop strategies that incorporate both sensuality and safety into the experience of those with whom we work.

Enabling sensuality at the same time as ensuring safety (in the intimate and personal care of others) might seem impossible. The sensual aspect of an experience is often reduced in the name of ensuring safety. We can become worried that a sensual experience is too sexual. However, lack of emotional and sensual experiences might leave the person with learning disabilities more vulnerable to abuse. Through lack of experience the person with learning disabilities may not be able to tell the difference between a safe and an unsafe experience at an early stage.

A lack of sensual experience might also lead to a lack of opportunity to express preference and personal boundaries and for these to be respected. This might also lead to a lack of opportunity for people with learning disabilities to respect preference and personal boundaries of others including other service users and carers. It is important for carers and service users not to overstep personal and organisational boundaries, but it is equally important to value the sensory experience and to provide opportunities for people to learn and respect personal and organisational boundaries.

Key Principles

- Sensuality is an important part of the quality of life for people with learning disabilities.

- Enabling sensual aspects of an activity for people with learning disabilities does not endanger safe working practices.

Training

The issue of sensuality should be explored with all staff within an organisation. Opportunity to explore these issues needs to be provided within a safe environment, for example, during a training day within group discussion.

Further Reading

Ellis, R; Naylor, L; (1997); **Sensuality and Safety from Training to Protect**; A compendium of Training Resources (in preparation). The Ann Craft Trust, University of Nottingham.

If concerns remain

If an individual worker has any concerns about what they are planning to do in terms of increasing sensual experiences, they need to talk to their manager. It is recommended that any procedure to enhance sensuality is recorded in the case notes and that at least two people are aware of the procedure within the organisation.

15. SEXUAL ORIENTATION

Underpinning knowledge

Everyone has the right, *within the law*, to express their sexuality in the way they choose and to identify themselves in the way that feels most comfortable to them.

Some adults with learning disabilities will identify themselves as lesbian, gay, bisexual, transvestite or transsexual. Staff must accept their identity and where relevant their choice of partner providing the relationship is a mutual one and not abusive or coercive.

Key Principles

Sexual orientation should be included in an Employer's Equal Opportunities Policy and, if so, state it is a disciplinary offence for staff to discriminate against anyone because of their sexual orientation. Staff should offer the same degree of support and respect to everyone.

Staff should also try to ensure that people are not subjected to prejudice or abuse (verbal or physical) by others and any complaint relating to such discrimination should be treated seriously.

Staff should remember that people are not always open and may be uncertain about their sexual orientation. Any 'disclosure' or even hints must be treated as confidential, unless permission is given by the service user to share the information for a specific reason or where abuse is suspected/evident.

Staff should avoid making stereotypical assumptions about a person's sexual orientation based upon dress, mannerisms, appearance etc. Staff should resist labelling people within sexual types unless they specifically choose this.

Training/Further Reading

Employer's Equal Opportunities Policies and Training.

Gunn, M J; (1996); **Sex and the Law**; (4th Edition); Family Planning Association, London.

Other Law (See Section 1)
● Of particular note the *Criminal Justice and Public Order Act 1994*. Staff should ensure that male services users are made aware that homosexual behaviour is illegal under the age of 18.

Even over the age of 18 it is illegal for homosexual behaviour to occur in a public place – *this would include the toilets in a day centre*.

●   There is no *law* which specifically relates to sexual acts between women.

Section 28 of the Local Government Act 1988 prohibits a local authority from intentionally promoting homosexuality or from publishing material with the intention of promoting homosexuality. It also allows courts to decide upon the intentions of the local authority if presented with evidence in connection with the abuse.

If concerns remain
Discuss with your line manager.

16. SELF STIMULATION

Underpinning knowledge

Self-stimulation, or masturbation, is a natural and healthy pleasurable activity.

Knowledge of, familiarity and comfort with, one's own body is intrinsically linked to positive self-esteem.

Key Principles

Masturbation is a private activity. Some adults with learning disabilities may benefit from staff assistance in differentiating between 'private' and 'public' places. (See Part 5, Staff Support).

People with learning disabilities should not be prevented from, or made to feel guilty about, masturbation because of personal values and attitudes held by individual members of staff.

Some people experience difficulty in masturbating. This can be due to a broad range of factors. The following are examples of some of the possible causes.

1. Psychological factors such as guilt or anxiety.

2. Physiological factors such as poor circulation, skin infections or inflammations, poor vaginal lubrication, and as a consequence of a number of physical disabilities.

3. Medical factors, including the side-effects of some prescribed medications, and the effects of some medications prescribed expressly to inhibit male erection.

4. Socioeconomic and environmental factors, including a lack of privacy and an absence of information and understanding.

People who experience difficulty in masturbating should, with their consent, be referred either via their GP or directly to generic sexual health services. The support of a key worker or other trusted person may be helpful in assisting the service user access such services.

No individual member of staff should ever attempt independently to teach people to masturbate. Where it is a clearly identified need that a person requires teaching input in order to masturbate effectively a multi-disciplinary meeting should be convened. The meeting should involve senior managers, and may also include medical professionals. Every effort should be made to involve the person in a meaningful way, preferably by his or her direct presence. Alternative means may involve recorded or videotaped statements to ensure views are not misrepresented.

Masturbation is a private and personal issue. However, it is important for both the protection of the adult with learning disabilities and involved workers that decisions regarding teaching in the area of masturbation should be reached by consensus. This will help to ensure both a transparency of process and ownership of agreed decisions at senior management level within involved services.

The outcome of the multi-disciplinary meeting will result in the formulation of a written Care Plan or protocol which will detail how, by whom, where and when any such teaching is undertaken; how the process will be monitored and evaluated, and by whom.

Unless specifically contracted to do so, it is highly unlikely that direct care staff would be responsible for delivering such teaching.

Training

As part of Induction Training all staff should receive input which encourages them to explore their individual values and attitudes in respect to issues of sexuality, and the potential tensions between these and effective professional practice.

Reading

Carson, D; (1992); **Legality of Responding to the Sexuality of a Client with Profound Learning Disabilities**; Mental Handicap 20, pp 85-87.

Downs, C; Craft, A; (1997); **Sex in Context Parts One and Two**; Pavilion Publications/Joseph Rowntree Foundation.

Gunn, M J; (1996); **Sex and the Law**; (4th Edition); Family Planning Association, London

Hingsburger, D; (1994); **Masturbation: A consultation for those who support individuals with development disabilities**; The Canadian Journal of Human Sexuality 3, pp 278-282.

Thompson, R; (Ed.) (1993); **Religious, Ethnicity, Sex Education; Exploring The Issues**; National Children's Bureau.

Gunn, M J; (1988); **Sex Education: an important decision**; Mental Handicap 16, 3.

Shelton, D; (1992); **Client sexual behaviour and Staff Attitudes**; Mental Handicap, 20, 2.

Downs, C; (1996); **A practical response to masturbation: working with people with profound and multiple disabilities**; Tizard Learning Disability Review, 1, 4.

If concerns remain
Discuss with your line manager or at the multi-disciplinary planning meeting.

17. SEXUAL HEALTH

Underpinning knowledge

Sexual health is a delicate area of work which needs to be sensitively and competently tackled. There are a range of agencies and specialist health staff available within mainstream NHS services.

Key Principles

- People with learning disabilities will need sufficient information to understand about the following issues:

  - At what stage of a man or woman's life they are fertile

  - Under what circumstances conception occurs

  - When the use of contraception might be appropriate

  - When sterilisation might be appropriate

  - How sterilisation works and its permanence

  - How infections are transmitted

  - How sexual infections are transmitted

  - How the risk of sexual infection might be reduced

  - The symptoms of sexual infections

  - Other genital conditions, not necessarily sexually transmitted (e.g. thrush and cystitis)

  - Where to get further information about genital conditions and sexual transmitted infections (including HIV and Aids).

- As people with learning disabilities may need assistance in accessing mainstream sexual health services, staff working with them need to be proactive in developing links.

Training

Staff need to be aware of the appropriate services and agencies available.

Reading/Resources

A range of information can be obtained from your local Family Planning Association.

If concerns remain

If concerns remain, these should be raised with the line manager or via the multi-disciplinary planning meeting.

18. CONTRACEPTION

Underpinning knowledge

People may wish to make decisions about contraception whether they are in a relationship or not.

The implications of an unwanted pregnancy are significant.

Some forms of contraception may be used for other purposes e.g. the contraceptive pill may be used to regulate periods, barrier methods may be used to reduce the risk of sexually transmitted diseases. (See Sexual Health.)

Key Principles

- People may wish to make a decision about contraception themselves or they may wish to make a decision with their partner. It should be made clear that if there is the possibility of pregnancy through a sexual relationship then both parties have responsibility for contraception.

- Decisions around the use of contraception should be based upon the informed choice of the person with learning disabilities and if they require assistance should be part of the multi-disciplinary approach.

- People should have choices as to where they go for information and who supports them in finding out the information. Gender may be an issue e.g. who provides the information, who provides any support or advocacy.

- Information about contraception is available from a range of health providers including both GP's nurses and Family Planning Agencies. Where possible, people with learning disabilities should be encouraged to access these services. They may need support to do this.

- People may require more than one session of advice and information

- The agencies providing the advice should be encouraged to produce information in accessible formats for people with learning disabilities. If this is not readily available then the person requiring the information should be given that information as soon as possible by whoever has access to it. However, the agencies that are responsible for providing contraceptive advice should be asked for accessible information to be available in the future.

- Practical issues around the use of contraception may need to be discussed with those people it affects e.g. if the contraceptive pill is used where it is kept and when it is taken. These issues should be noted on care plans where appropriate.

- Staff need to maintain confidentiality (see Part 8) over matters to do with contraception.

- Family members may have views about contraception and their family member with learning disabilities. These only need to be taken into account if the person with learning disabilities requests it.

Training

Identified staff need training around the issues of contraception, unwanted pregnancy and pregnancy.

Reading/Resources

A range of information is available from your local Family Planning Association or Brook Advisory Centre.

If concerns remain
Discuss with your line manager.

19. PREGNANCY AND UNWANTED PREGNANCY

Underpinning knowledge

Pregnancy and the desire to be or not to be pregnant are not always straightforward matters.

Guidelines such as these can only give pointers as to how best to enable people to gain information, make informed choices and act on those decisions.

Key Principles

- Individuals and couples may need someone independent of any service that they receive to discuss issues relating to pregnancy.

- Staff may need to support people in accessing specialist services including counselling.

- People with learning disabilities planning to have a child will need support and advice. It is important that such support is planned within a multi-disciplinary context.

- Staff may well need additional support when working in this area. Support within and outside the agency should be established early on.

Reading/Resources

A range of information is available from your local Family Planning Clinic or Brook Advisory Service as well as from local NHS services.

If concerns remain
Concerns should be discussed with your line manager or via the multi-disciplinary team.

20. STERILISATION AND VASECTOMY

Underpinning knowledge

Sterilisation covers both the sterilisation of women and vasectomy for men. However, for people with learning disabilities, it is often thought to be an issue for women. Therefore, this section will include both terms i.e. sterilisation and vasectomy. The word sterilisation will apply to women only.

People choose to have sterilisations and vasectomies because they never want to become pregnant or to become parents. This decision can be reached for a number of reasons. For people without disabilities doctors are loath to perform sterilisations or vasectomies on people in their early to mid-twenties. The assumption behind this is that people do change their minds. Women with learning disabilities have been and are sterilised in their teens and early twenties. There are, therefore, concerns around equal opportunities e.g. with regard to gender and disabilities, with this issue.

Women may be given a hysterectomy for ostensibly medical reasons e.g. heavy periods, fibroids. However, these days, such radical surgery is seen to be the last rather than the first resort for such conditions. Care needs to be taken that a medical reason is not being used for a social end e.g. to produce infertility.

Sterilisation and vasectomy are valued options for some people, whether they already have children or not. It is important that people make decisions within the context of their life – both in the present and in the future. Although some procedures may be reversible, it is safer to assume that sterilisation and vasectomy are permanent.

Sterilisation and vasectomy can be very traumatic events for the body. Other forms of contraception are less intrusive and injurious.

Key Principles

- No one should be sterilised or have a vasectomy without their foreknowledge.

- Care workers should not carry out any support in this area unaided. All decisions should be reached through a multi-disciplinary meeting.

- The decision around having a sterilisation or a vasectomy should be a valued choice by a person i.e. to enhance their life. It should not be made through fear.

- Sterilisation and vasectomy are long term answers. They should not be used in response to short term questions.

- The reasoning behind requests for sterilisation and vasectomy should be fully explored. If the request comes from a family member then it may be necessary to provide some support for the family from someone who does not have contact with the adult with learning disabilities.

- Decisions about sterilisation and vasectomy should generally be made after other less intrusive and less final contraception has been used.

- The person should be encouraged to use an independent advocate where sterilisation and vasectomy are being considered. The advocate must be involved at the earliest stage.

Training

Staff need access to specific information as and when required.

If concerns remain
Concerns should be discussed in the multi-disciplinary forum.

21. PARENTING

Underpinning knowledge

People with learning disabilities have the same rights as everyone to become parents. However, parenthood carries serious responsibilities and the needs of children are always paramount. This applies to everyone regardless of whether or not they have learning disabilities.

Parents with learning disabilities do encounter difficulties and a review of the literature (McGaw, 1993) revealed that often when such parents do not receive specific support and intensive teaching, their children are taken into care. Information and advice about parenting should be made available to people when it is needed or requested. Some people with learning disabilities may need counselling to explore their expectations and to assess their parenting capacities. Some people with specific disabilities may require practical assistance in looking after any children and this may be provided as part of a care package based on assessed need.

Many people with learning disabilities will be as capable as the rest of us of providing a loving and nurturing environment for children. However, under the Children's Act 1989, where the welfare of the child is thought to be at risk, the Social Services Department has a duty to intervene.

For some people with learning disabilities who want to become parents, conception may not be possible or may be unlikely. These people may need specific counselling and should be referred to agencies that can provide professional advice and support. In these situations it is important to be realistic and not raise unrealistic expectations among the individuals concerned.

Key Principles

- People with learning disabilities have the same rights as everyone to become parents.

- The literature reveals (McGaw, 1993) that children of parents with learning disabilities are 'at risk' from developmental delay and learning disabilities. It is therefore important to assess the parental competency of people with learning disabilities who have children and provide the necessary support, particularly in the areas of practical skills and of social skills.

Training

Staff working with parents with learning disabilities will need to access specific training.

Further Reading

Llewellyn, G; (1997); **Parents with Intellectual Disability learning to parent. The role of experience and informal learning**; International Journal of Disability, Development and Education, Volume 44, No. 3.

McGaw, S; (1993); **Working with parents on parenting skills. In Parents with Learning Disabilities**; BILD Seminar Papers No. 3.

McGaw, S; Sturmey, P; (1993); **Identifying the needs of parents with Learning Disabilities**; A Review. Child Abuse Review, Volume 2: pp 101-117.

McGaw, S; Sturmey, P; (1993); **Identifying the needs of parents with Learning Disabilities**; The parental skills model; Child Abuse Review, Volume 3: pp 36-51.

McGaw, S; (1997); **Practical support for parents with Learning Disabilities. In Adults with Learning Disabilities**; O'Hara, J; Sperlinger, A; (Eds); John Wiley and Sons Limited.

If concerns remain

A referral to the Social Services Department may be necessary for the provision of intensive support in order to ensure the safety of the children.

22. MARRIAGE AND OTHER PARTNERSHIPS

Underpinning knowledge

Anyone over the age of 18 can marry someone of the opposite sex without parental permission. As no one can consent to marriage on behalf of another person, it is up to the registrar to be satisfied that the partners to be married understand the nature of the contract they are about to undertake.

All adults with learning disabilities have the right to marry, if they wish.

Key Principles

- Some people with learning disabilities may need assistance in understanding the responsibilities of marriage and staff may need to provide them with whatever assistance and information they need, so that they can make an informed choice. Residential provision should reflect the wishes of the partnership.

- Some staff, relatives/carers or other service users may have moral or religious objections to sexual relationships outside marriage. Those concerned may need help to work through these differences of view or objections. However, moral and religious codes not shared by the couple concerned should not be imposed upon them.

- People working with people with learning disabilities should also work within their Employer's policies and guidelines, including Equal Opportunities Policy.

- Staff should encourage people to access mainstream services such as Relate where necessary.

If concerns remain
Discuss with line manager.

23. DIVORCE AND SEPARATION

Underpinning knowledge

It must be recognised that any relationship no matter how long it has been in existence can break up. This will be no different for people with learning disabilities. In such situations staff need to be equipped to provide the appropriate support and guidance but only at the request of one or both parties. If staff suspect one of the partners is being abused then appropriate action should be taken in accordance with their Vulnerable Adults Policy.

Key Principles

- Staff should not attempt to persuade the couple to either part or stay together. The decision to part is ultimately for the two people concerned.

- Counselling/support from outside agencies e.g. Relate, should be offered to the individual.

Training

- Vulnerable Adult Procedures/Domestic Violence Policies.

- Information pertaining to agencies, counselling services within local area who can offer support/guidance to couples whose relationship is breaking down e.g. Relate.

If concerns remain
Discuss with line manager.

24. SEXUALLY STIMULATING MATERIAL

Underpinning knowledge

Many adults choose to view or use sexually stimulating materials, often as an aid to masturbation or other forms of sexual activity. Sexually stimulating materials may include newspapers, mail order catalogues, magazines, books, videos, pictures, and specialist telephone services. Some of this kind of material is sometimes referred to as 'soft porn' or 'top shelf' and is legally available to adults, others are generally available.

Whatever an individual member of staff's feelings about such material, it is important to distinguish it from materials which would breach the Obscene Publications Act. These materials would, for example, feature illegal sexual activities, often involving children, animals or torture.

It is illegal to purchase or own these sorts of materials. It is also an offence to obtain such material for others.

Key Principles

- While staff may have a responsibility to support a service user who wishes to access such material, they also have a responsibility to explain issues of privacy in regard to its use, the offence it may cause to others, and the legal context of such material (e.g. not showing it to minors).

- Staff must not promote or initiate the introduction of sexually stimulating material to an adult with learning disability.

- Services should ensure that people who wish to access or purchase sexually stimulating material do so discreetly and confine its use to within the privacy of their own rooms. (See 'House Rules' in Part 5 'Staff Support')

Training

As part of Induction Training, all staff should receive input which encourages them to explore their personal values and attitudes in respect to issues of sexuality and the potential tensions between these and effective professional practice.

Reading

McCarthy, M; Thompson, D; (Revised 1998); **Sex and the three Rs. Rights, responsibilities and risks: A sex education package for working with people with learning difficulties.** Pavilion Publishing, Hove.

Thompson, D; Brown, H; (1998); **Response – Ability;** Pavilion Publications/ Mental Health Foundation.

Thompson, R; (Ed.); (1993); **Religion, Ethnicity, Sex Education: Exploring the Issues;** National Children's Bureau.

NB. There appears to be no published research regarding the use and effects of sexually stimulating material by and on adults with learning disabilities. Most published research focuses on the sex offender population, and therefore does not deal with service users who use such material and do not commit sexual offences.

If concerns remain

If staff are unclear or concerned about the possible consequences of a service user accessing sexually stimulating material, a multi-disciplinary risk assessment should be undertaken.

Factors to be considered in such a risk assessment would include:

- the service users' existing sexual values, attitudes and knowledge; including their capacity to realise such material may well cause offence to others

- their capacity to comprehend the 'fantasy' element often present in such material

- whether they previously or presently display sexually inappropriate or abuse towards others

- their capacity, and the service's support, to ensure such material is used and kept privately.

It may well be helpful for staff to involve an outside specialist, such as a clinical psychologist, in the assessment of such factors.

25. SEXUAL ABUSE

Underpinning knowledge

Sexual abuse includes behaviours which are illegal (e.g. rape and harassment) and behaviours for which no specific offence is outlined in law (e.g. persistent invasion of other's personal space).

Sexual abuse can involve both:

1. Contact abuse: touch, e.g. of breast, genitals, anus, mouth; masturbation of either or both persons; penetration or attempted penetration of vagina, anus, or mouth, with or by penis, fingers or objects.

2. Non-contact abuse; 'being encouraged or made to look at pornographic materials, obscene telephone calls, indecent exposure, serious teasing or innuendo'. (Brown and Turk, 1992).

Children aren't the only victims of sexual abuse. Due to a range of factors, adults with learning disabilities are more likely to be victims of sexual abuse than other sections of the population. Such factors include:

1. Pervasive lack of privacy and dependence on paid staff and other family members;

2. Lack of knowledge and skills to recognise abuse and/or assert themselves in the face of abuse.

3. Possible communication difficulties, including an absence of vocabulary to describe body parts/sexual behaviour. Professionals from other agencies, such as the Police and the Crown Prosecution Service, may also be wary of service users' capacity to act as 'reliable witnesses'.

4. Credibility perceptions on the part of staff and/or other family members regarding adults with learning disabilities' capacity for confabulation, suggestibility and 'attention seeking'.

We are aware from research that the vast majority of sexual abuse is perpetrated by men. Often the perpetrator is a male relative or close family friend. He may be another adult with learning disabilities or someone in a position of trust and/or power. For example, a manager, care worker, advocate, volunteer or taxi driver.

It is important that staff recognise that male service users can be perpetrators of sexual abuse.

Key Principles

- All services should have a clear and effective Sexual Abuse Policy and Procedures for staff to follow. Staff Procedures will include a framework for responding to concerns, allegations and disclosures.

- A robust Sexual Abuse Policy will help to ensure everyone connected with the service is aware of the possibility of abuse occurring. Adults with learning disabilities will know they will be listened to. Parents and Carers will be aware of the vigilance exercised within the service. Staff will know what to do in the event of concerns or allegations being made. Abusers are less likely to attempt to perpetrate abuse.

Possible Signs & Symptoms of Sexual Abuse

1. Medical/forensic – where medical help is needed and a medical problem could be related to sexual abuse, either as a direct consequence of abuse or as a related side effect, e.g. a vaginal infection, or someone is complaining of soreness between her legs.

2. Behavioural/emotion – sudden, new or unexplained marked changes in behaviour, e.g. disturbed sleep, or the person appears to be depressed for no apparent reason.

3. Circumstantial – a piece of evidence that tends to support an allegation or suspicion, e.g. discarded or hidden torn underwear.

4. Disclosure/witness – when somebody tells you that something has occurred, or you witness it happening, e.g. saying someone 'Did rude things to me'.

NB. The above list is far from exhaustive. Neither does the occurrence of one or a number of such factors *prove* sexual abuse has occurred. The presence of such factors or concerns should, however, trigger staff to pursue their service's Sexual Abuse Procedures.

Some people who have been or are being abused will not display any of the type of signs and symptoms referred to above.

Staff should not seek to deny or minimise the impact of sexual abuse on a person because of their learning disability.

Adults with learning disabilities who are victims of sexual abuse have the same rights to redress within the law as other members of the public. They also have the same entitlement of access to generic counselling and therapeutic services available for all victims of sexual abuse.

While it is not the responsibility of staff to provide counselling, they have a key role in ensuring adults with learning disabilities are aware of such opportunities, and support their access. Advocates also have a potential role to play in ensuring people receive appropriate support.

Services should encourage links with agencies such as the Police and generic abuse support and counselling services as part of their preparedness for responding to instances of sexual abuse.

Adults with learning disabilities who perpetrate sexual abuse have a right to a service. Often they are not prosecuted for their offences, or receive non-custodial outcomes from the criminal justice system. They should have the same opportunity for assessment and treatment as mainstream offenders. Again the role of an advocate may be helpful in ensuring the abuser receives appropriate services.

The rights of people who perpetrate sexual abuse should not, however, compromise the safety or well-being of their peers, or staff.

Training

As part of the Induction Training all staff should receive training regarding their service's Sexual Abuse Policy and Staff Procedures. Such training should recognise that just as adults with learning disabilities may or will be victims of sexual abuse, the same is likely to be true for some members of staff.

References and Reading

Brown, J; Turk, V; (1992); **Defining Sexual Abuse as it affects Adults with Learning Disabilities**; Mental Handicap 20, 2, 44-55.

Churchill, J; Craft, A; Holding, A; Horrocks, C; (Eds); (1996); **It Could Never Happen Here**; ARC/NAPSAC.

Churchill, J; Brown, J; Craft, A; Horrocks, C; (Eds); (1997); **There Are No Easy Answers**; ARC/NAPSAC.

Gunn, M J; (1996); **Sex and the Law**; Family Planning Association, London.

Sobsey, D; (1994); **Violence and Abuse in the lives of People with Disabilities: The End of Silent Acceptance?** Paul H. Brookes Publishing Company.

Thompson, D; Brown, H; (1998); **Response – Ability**; Pavilion Publications/ Mental Health Foundation

If concerns remain

The following agencies have extensive experience of working with issues of sexual abuse and people with learning disabilities, and can provide guidance and information for staff who have concerns in those areas.

The Ann Craft Trust (formerly NAPSAC), University of Nottingham, Centre for Social Work, University Park, Nottingham, NG7 2RD
Telephone 0115 951 5400

Respond, 3rd Floor, 24-32 Stephenson Way, London, NW1 2HD
Telephone 0207 383 0700
Helpline 0845 606 1503 Monday to Friday 1.30 pm – 5 pm

Voice UK., PO Box 238, Derby DE1 9JN
Telephone 01332 519 872

26. SERVICE STANDARDS

Underpinning knowledge

Authorities agreeing a policy on Personal and Social Relationships will not, in itself, ensure that adults with learning disabilities are effectively supported in those relationships. As with all policies, it is essential that this is incorporated into service specifications and contracts.

Key Principles

- Once a Policy is agreed, all providers of services must be made aware of the policy and its contents. It is advised that all Providers of services are able to access training.

- All Service Specifications, Contracts and Service Level Agreements should specify that compliance with the Policy is mandatory.

- Each service should have a nominated member of staff who takes the lead responsibility for ensuring the policy is implemented.

- Contract monitoring arrangements should ensure that the Policy is implemented and that managers and staff are aware of it. Failure to comply should be addressed within the authorities' usual contracting procedure.

- Care Managers should ensure that the Policy is implemented in relation to individuals they are responsible for. Any perceived failure to comply should be reported to the appropriate contracting forum in line with the Authorities' normal procedure.

- All services should include guidance on relationships and expectations about behaviours in the Information Leaflet for service users and their carers so that these are clear (Please also refer to Part 5 on Staff Support).

Training

Should be part of the Induction training for new staff.

If concerns remain
Discuss with the local Registration and Inspection Unit or Social Services Health Authority Contracts Section.